T0116893

My Life's Treasures...

To Review and Consider Later!

A book of

Poetry and Prose

By

Kathleen Luksza Morrissey

With contributions

From

Shaun P. Morrissey

Melissa Mathews

And

James F. Plummer

authorHOUSE

AuthorHouse™
1663 Liberty Drive
Bloomington, IN 47403
www.authorhouse.com
Phone: 1-800-839-8640

First published by AuthorHouse 5/10/2011

ISBN: 978-1-4567-2206-7 (sc)
ISBN: 978-1-4567-2205-0 (e)

Library of Congress Control Number: 2011900313

Printed in the United States of America
Bloomington, Indiana

This book is printed on acid-free paper.

This book is dedicated to all my life's treasures...
the people in my life past and present who've made me who I am.

It is most especially dedicated to my son Terry L. Morrissey,
Who died suddenly in a motorcycle accident in August, 2010.

And my dear husband Jack Morrissey, who suffered greatly
and lost his battle with cancer in 2009.

My niece Patti Zarzeck who suffered greatly,
and lost her battle with cancer earlier last year.

My dear friend Laura Chaklos who died suddenly
in an automobile accident last year.

And my parents Louis and Mary Luksza, who always believed in me, and started me
on this journey, giving me the courage and fortitude to withstand the losses!

I've laughed with them and I've cried with them!
I miss them and I'll love them, always!

And to my son Shaun Morrissey, who holds my heart in his hands,
and gives me a reason to go on!

My brothers and all my sisters of the heart!

All of my dear friends...
Especially Jim

The great loves of my life...

Kathleen Luksza Morrissey

Contents

My Life's Treasure

I struggle with the concept, after passing's observed...
Is it easier to go quickly, suddenly, and not know?
Can you slip from this world into the next
With no pain, no suffering, no long and sad goodbyes?
Are you spared the hurt of letting go,
of accepting that life's journey has ended?
Are you suddenly face to face with all those
Who had gone before, so filled with joy to see them
That you don't notice that you left...
And If you know before you go, and have time
To say goodbye, if you suffer greatly,
Review the life you've had...Make peace with disappointments,
Get over your regrets...
Say I'm sorry if it's needed, I love you to a few...
I'm so happy that our paths crossed...and I'll be missing you!
Is it easier to have your loved ones help you on your way,
And then reach out to those who've come to get you,
and slowly drift away...
I don't know the answer, don't know God's plan for me...
And so I try to live my life so there are few regrets,
I try to know what is important... and ultimately what isn't!
I try to say I'm sorry, or I forgive you, If need be...
I try to say I love you to my friends and family,
And to that special someone... at every opportunity...
I've never seen the ocean...never had moneys to spare!
Never done so many things... and maybe never will...
But my life has been blessed by the people who've graced it,
The love, the laughter, the sheer joy of the dance...
And what could be better than that!
When they come to take me home, if I haven't said goodbye...
If I've ever said I love you, if I've hugged you,
If I've laughed...Or if I've cried with you...
Until we meet again...
Please know that you were my life, you were my treasures...
I'm holding your hand, I'm holding you in my heart...forever!
My sons, my family, my friends...my love!
Kathleen Luksza Morrissey

Terry Morrissey...

A guy with an outstanding appreciation for nice shirts,
the original owner of the mysterious missing pants,
he could make another man's suit look like it was made for him,
dress shirts were white; ties were black,
...but otherwise, it was Wranglers, T-shirts, and black boots.
He wore a black motorcycle jacket and shades.
But what the casual observer didn't know was, tucked into the inside
pocket of that motorcycle jacket was his rosary, a gift from his mother...
and that the eyes behind those shades were gentle and kind.
He wore a smile always...that he put on just for you, his family, his
friends...
I don't know what they wear in Heaven, but I hope Laura greeted him,
looking stunning in her red dress, because I know he would've loved
seeing her in it, just one more time!

Melissa Mathews

Jack Morrissey's Wife

For thirty five years I had a wonderful life!
For thirty five years I was Jack Morrissey's wife!
If you didn't know him....
Wow! What to say!
He was stubborn and headstrong,
He was sweet and kind, and...hilarious!
He could tell a story or joke better than anyone!
Make you laugh till you cried!
Till you actually ached inside!
He was a good husband, a good dad, a great friend!
...And he was ALWAYS late!
You could be so angry with him!
And when he finally arrived...
Was he ever worth the wait!
He could take the most ordinary moment
And fill it with magic!
He was patriotic and conservative...
And oh so rebellious!
He made me see the world in a whole new way,
Changed the way I would look at an ordinary day!
So many told me that I was a "saint"
For putting up with him!
The truth of the matter is I loved him,
It was the joy of my life
And oh what a privilege...
To be Jack Morrissey's wife!

Kathleen Morrissey

Saying Goodbye

Saying goodbye is...something I never got to say!
Before I could, you had already gone away...
I did say I love you, and be careful, and I love you...
Each and every time we parted!
Life had already taught me that you never miss a chance...
It might be your only chance, your last chance,
your best chance...
To say I love you, and so...
They were my last words to you, that day,
The day we didn't know that you would go away!
and yours to me..."Love you too, Mommy!"
Will live in my heart forever,
In my heart...where you will always be...
In my heart...where I will never say goodbye!

Kathleen Luksza Morrissey

For my son, Terry Morrissey

To Review and Consider Later

Whenever something is on my mind, or in my heart...
I write it down...I tell it...
to review and consider later!
Sometimes I send it to my special friend,
I've worn him out I'm afraid...bearing my soul, my heart,
my yearnings and pain!
And sometimes my warped sense of humor!
And then I wonder if he knows that he should laugh, or smile...
At the satire of us!
Does he get it?
Does he review and consider later?
Sometimes I don't share it with anyone at all,
writing it was enough, saying it to me...
to review and consider later!
It is the therapy of my mind, of my heart and soul...
To put it down on paper!
When something is bothering me, hurting me,
and the pain won't go away...
When something is pleasing me,
making my heart sing!
I write it down...
to review and consider later!
It is my own brand of therapy, my survival kit,
Sometimes it saves my sanity...
And often it documents my insanity...
To review and consider later!

Kathleen Luksza Morrissey

Shaun

From the time you were born
To this very day
"A chip off the old block"
Is what some would say...
So like your dad in so many ways!
And a little like me, I find...
And yet you are so unique,
So special, so funny, so thoughtful, so kind!
Your outlook on life so amusing!
You always seem to entertain...
Being around you is a pleasure!
When all the clouds are darkening my day
You are the sunshine that lights the way!
You hold your sorrow deep inside
You won't let pain destroy you!
I hope you know
You are my most precious treasure...
And just how much I love you!

For my son Shaun P. Morrissey

Kathleen Luksza Morrissey

Thank You

My heart overflows with gratitude
for all of you who care!
I'm overwhelmed with the love
and compassion, and friendship
you've given...
It keeps me sane!
When I want to give up,
crawl away someplace, beaten by life,
Torn to shreds, lost in the pain of losing...
One of you is always there...
my family, my friends,
family of my heart...
listening, hugging, offering a smile,
Kindness, caring...
sending a card, a text message, a call...
and best of all sharing
some sweet silly, memory,
which can make me smile...
When I think of my sweet Terry!
If it takes a village to raise a child
It takes a metropolis to bury !

Thank you all so much
For loving me,
for loving him...
For caring!

Kathleen Luksza Morrissey

A Gift of Love

I gave you me as a gift of love.
I changed myself for you;
I changed my thoughts, my words, my actions...
Until I was only a reflection of who you are!
Now there is no more left of myself;
My self confidence
My self pride
Or my self respect...
There is nothing left for me to give to you.
I never knew before that I liked the old me so much!
Now, I need to go back!
Maybe there is still a little of the innocence
At the other end of the road...
This doesn't mean that I don't love you anymore...
It only means that my heart and soul
Are yearning for the me I used to be...
And I have to say goodbye!

Kathleen Luksza Morrissey

A Partner for the Dance

You make me laugh when I feel like crying...
You make me smile through my tears!
You don't understand that inside I'm dying...
You don't understand my fears!
You want me to dance and be happy!
I want to ball up and hide...
I can't be who you want...
I can't be who you need...
That part of me has died!
And yet I keep reaching for your optimism...
I remember how it felt!
When tomorrow was full of promise
And every day was new!
Hope was...love around the corner...
A partner for the dance!
You make me laugh when I feel like crying...
You make me smile through my tears!
I wish I'd met you sooner...
When tomorrow was full of promise
And everyday day was new...
Hope was love around the corner...
A partner for the dance!
When tomorrow could be full of promise...
If it was spent with you!

Kathy Morrissey

A Test of Faith

I wish I understood how I came to be in this place...
If I met God face to face could he explain it to me?
They tell me he never gives us more than we can bear
And yet I think there are asylums full of people...
Who would beg to differ!
Every time he closes a door he opens a window...
Is the window supposed to be for my great escape?
Are the footsteps in the sand where he carried me...
Right up to the jagged cliff,
Only to dump me into the deep end of the ocean?
If I begged him for his mercy,
would he finally give me peace?
Or, would he tell me I'd been too blessed ,
And he was only making an adjustment to correct
What I shouldn't have had to begin with?
Is it a test of my faith?
If it is...
I've passed with flying colors!
I still believe!
God gives...and he takes away!
He sacrificed his Son to save my soul...
And he took mine, to destroy it!

Kathy Morrissey

An Angel Among Us

God has blessed me with the gift of love!
It all began when my mom loved my dad,
And my brothers and sisters and me...
And if that wasn't enough...
she had room in her heart to love
Anyone who needed it...
Anyone who needed a place to go
Or a meal to hold them,
A shoulder to cry on ...
Or a gentle touch, or word or smile!
She was the best and strongest person
I've ever known...an angel among us!
She was the glue, the backbone of our family!
If I've had doubts that God loves me,
When life is breaking my heart...
I just remember he gave me my mom...
She taught me to love...
She taught me to have strong shoulders
And a gentle heart...
And was an angel among us!

For my Mom, Mary Luksza
Kathleen Luksza Morrissey

Coming Together

We just keep saying goodbye...and then coming together!
Each time I want to cry...and think it is forever!
Will I ever stop loving you?
Will you ever stop wanting me?
Will the needs that we share...
Ever set us free?
You say that we can never be, and yet...
We just keep saying goodbye...and then coming together!
Each time I want to cry...and think it is forever!
Will I love you still on my dying day?
Will you want me still when I'm old and grey?
Will the needs that we share...
Ever set us free?
You say that we can never be,
and yet...
We just keep saying goodbye...and then coming together!

Kathleen Luksza Morrissey

Do You Care?

Do you care that I love you
And know I was wrong?
Do you feel as I do...
That we've been apart too long?

Do you care that I miss you,
And the way you loved me?
If I could only kiss you...
Then would you see?

Do you care that I'm sorry
And that I can cry too?
Will you only forgive me,
And let me make it up to you?

Do you care?

Kathy Luksza Morrissey

Do you remember me?

Not the me I am today...
But the me I used to be?
She is just a vague memory!
She felts things...too much,
cried too easily!
She was soft and tender,
compassionate, kind!
She died a slow and agonizing death,
and this other person lives in her body now!
I'm not sure who she is...
she doesn't cry easily,
and she laughs too much!
She doesn't seem to have a conscience, really!
Well maybe a little,
She doesn't want to hurt anybody,
she doesn't believe in pain!
She'll do just about anything
to hang onto someone she loves
or thinks she loved once,
when she could still feel...

Kathy Morrissey

Do you remember?

Do you remember what it was like ...to fall in love...
Do you remember the first time?

The excitement! The anticipation! The hope!
The fear, the anxiety, the uncertainty...
Do you remember the passion...
The heat of desire, the touching, the needing...
And how it consumed you?

You feel it ...the falling, in the pit of your stomach
In the fluttering of your heart, in the heat deep inside,
The desire to know, to please, to lose ...yourself...

I remember it well, though it happened long ago!
It filled my life, it made me whole...

Do you remember what it was like ...to fall in love...
Do you remember the last time?
Do you remember the passion...
The heat of desire, the touching, the needing...
And how it consumed you?

You feel it... the falling, in the pit of your stomach
In the fluttering of your heart, in the heat deep inside,
The desire to know, to please, to lose yourself...

I'd almost forgotten, and then,
I remember it well, it's happening again...!

The excitement! The anticipation! The hope!
The fear, the anxiety, the uncertainty...
Do you remember what it is like ...to fall in love?

Kathleen Luksza Morrissey

Dreams..

Dreams come to us all naturally, some simple, and others bazaar!
Dreamed about close ones, and others we know not of from afar..

She dreamed of having a Prince on his white horse, and holding the silver sword..
He dreamed of sharing love with a Princess, and knowing she was sent from the Lord..

We dreamed our dreams hoping to realize them true one day...
But when we vision what appeared, why do we let it slip away?

Allow your pillow to absorb your thoughts, and all you dreamed during the night..
Forget the nightmares that appeared , and know your next dream will be full of light..

Each mind, and heart acts within,
and attempts to direct us on our course..
But if we don't achieve, then say a prayer, and ask:
"Lord I want you to become my force"..

The Lord will answer, and send you a special dream..
Open your eyes, and let your knight vision your gleam..

James F. Plummer

Enough

Why is it enough for you...
The moments that we share?
Stolen moments spent together-
Talking, sharing, laughing,
Loving, passion, caring,
touching...longing...
I wish it was enough for me!
I live for the moments
spent with you...
The moments that we share!
Stolen moments spent together
When you are wanting me!
If it is all you have to give...
Then can it be enough for me?

Kathy Morrissey

Even Before

Even before I heard you speak...
Even before your hand touched mine,
your words, written, sent, treasured...
Spoke to me, touched a place long denied,
and I almost loved you from the start!

Even before your eyes met mine,
Even before our lips touched,
Our bodies joined, our souls united,
I knew, somewhere inside of me...
That you and I would want to be!

Even before I fell I knew ...

That someday I would love you!

Kathleen Luksza Morrissey

Finding

There are times when the sadness, the regrets in life are
overwhelming, and The disappointments more than you can bear!
The sorrow that stays with you throughout the day, blocks the sun,
Hides the light, invades your sleep, and lengthens the night

It's then that you must make a choice, to stay in this hellish place
Finding some grim comfort in being wrapped in your misery
Or go forward, reaching once again cautiously, for happiness,
Letting someone in, taking a chance, having hope...Daring to love...

Finding there are still moments of joy, whispers of bliss,
Finding that life is worth living, hope is worth having...
 love is worth giving!

Kathleen Luksza Morrissey

For All Eternity

I want to be the one you say goodbye to...at the end!
I want you to kiss me...and hold onto my hand...
Look into my eyes and see that you were loved...
and tell me that you loved me too...almost from the start!
I want you to be proud that I was at your side...and in your heart...
I want you to feel that you finally got it right!
I want you to know that you could love... and did love well!
I want you to believe that we were meant to be...that
God brought us together...soul mates...for all eternity!

I want you to be the one I say goodbye to...at the end!
I want to kiss you...and hold onto your hand...
I want to look into your eyes and tell you that I loved you from the start...
That I was proud to have you by my side...and in my heart!
I want you to know that it always felt so right, and
I want to tell you just how much I loved you...
And that we were meant to be...
And that I thank God for bringing us together...
Soul mates... for all eternity!

I don't want us to say goodbye at all...until the very end!
I want us to grow old together, always young at heart...
The chemistry, the compatibility, the contentment always there...
Memories of our many years together we will share!
Until when we are very, very old, we part...
The fire that was between us, still an ember... glowing softly...
Lighting the way...Until we meet again...
Soul mates ...for all eternity!

Kathleen Luksza Morrissey

For Better or Worse

Can't get angry, I can't get sad...
Every stupid feeling that I've ever had...
It's all been done; It's all been felt... It's done!
Dance to a song I've never heard...
I'd sing along, but I don't know the words
It can't be done...It's all been done...It can't...

I kind of get the feeling,
something bad is about to happen ...
You know what I'm thinking...
I kind of think it should!
Smashed my faith...I killed my dreams!
Smashed my faith...I killed my dreams!

Hope will only make you weak!
Cures are worse than the disease...
I'm so sick, sick of everything!
Dance to a song I've never heard...
I'd sing along, but I don't know the words
It can't be done...It's all been done...It can't...

I kind of get the feeling,
Nothing new has ever happened...
At least not in my lifetime,
I really wish it would!

Lyrics by Shaun Morrissey (drummer)
Recorded by The Humanoids
The Humanoids Rule Earth

For Once and For All

I've always been in a hurry!
The romantic in me craving love...
I've always wanted to be treasured,
For once and for all and forever!
And I've given my heart
Too quickly...
Had it broken beyond measure!
I think I will take it slow this time,
Let it build...
Let friendship, laughter, and fun
Lead the way!
Let it ripen...
Ferment like a fine wine...
Develop slowly over time!
And the love that grows
Will be treasured...
For once, and for all, and forever!
Please don't ask me to hurry!
I have to mend, to heal...
It will be better I promise,
and well worth the wait...
the love that grows between us
Will be treasured...
For once, and for all, and forever!

Kathleen Luksza Morrissey

I Cannot Yet See

People who observe us together...
think we've been a couple forever!
They think you are my husband,
I am your wife!
They are seeing something...
that I cannot yet see!
It amuses me, and yet I wonder...
Are we meant to be?
I like you an awful lot...
You make me laugh
You make me smile...
You are good for me it seems!
And I love...dancing with you!
Are we meant to be?
Will you turn out to be...
my dance partner forever?
The last love of my life?
They are seeing something
that I cannot yet see!
Although I must admit...
I like the possibility!

Kathleen Luksza Morrissey

I Didn't Mean To

I didn't mean to hurt you,
That was never my intention!
I tried so hard to warn you,
You just wouldn't listen!
I told you I was in turmoil...
Not ready to fall in love!
I told you that I like you
And I do, an awful lot!
We've had such fun
I hate to run...
I'll miss you when I go!
Staying will only make it worse,
I lead you on it seems!
My signals are mixed
I must admit,
And it isn't fair to you!
I hope that you can forgive me,
And that you find another
Who will appreciate
The wonderfulness of you!
One day I may regret it
It is an awful thing to do...
But I can't give a heart that's aching,
And breaking...not for you!
I didn't know when I met you
That my world would soon fall apart!
And if I still had it in me
To fall in love with someone new,
I can guarantee for sure...
that someone
Would be you!

Kathleen Luksza Morrissey

I Know

I know I love you now,
And once you loved me too—
But I blew it for a dream
That I found couldn't come true!

And I know it's too late
To show you how I feel,
Yet I want you to know
That my love for you is real!

Sometimes I can't help but cry,
And now I feel so lonely—
But I guess I'll have to say
...goodbye...
Although I love you only!

Kathleen Luksza Morrissey
STA 73

I love...

Reading your e-mails (what ever happened to that guy? So like you, and yet different somehow) and poems (did I ever tell you "The Mirror" was my favorite?)
I love that we felt so natural together right from the start...
And I love listening to you talk, the sound of your voice,
and what you have to say as well! (Even if I don't always agree!)
I love your honesty, and your sense of humor...you make me smile!
I love eating a meal that you've prepared just for me! and
I love snuggling up next to you to watch TV,
 So content, relaxed, comfortable ...(sometimes so tired, too!)
I love the anticipation of discovering things I don't yet know about
you, and...
That you are, sometimes oddly, an "old fashioned guy"
Your taste in cars, and sitcoms...
I love it that you like baseball! GO CARDS!!!
I love that you refuse to go to the computer for the answer
during a "senior moment"! and That you think the lyrics to
 "When a man loves a woman" are dumb...
Who would ask someone they love to sleep out in the rain anyway?
I love it that your "dream" woman is some crazy hippy chick
version of "Aunt Jamima"!
I love it when you call me "Hon"...And the way you kiss me
(virtual kisses too, to start the day! What ever happened to that guy
anyway?)
I love that you're a romantic, and passionate and
I love the way you make me feel- young, and sexy, and alive!
 I love your hands stroking, your tongue teasing, and
The way you make me feel inside!
I love kissing, touching, craving... you!
And I love how you turn into someone else
 ...The look in your eyes, on your face...
The sweet little lies, Oh how I wish them true!
 and the way I have to swim back thru the fog
  to comprehend what you are saying...and OMG!
what you are saying! I love how You excite me!

But, I don't love you, ...not yet...not totally and completely...

I'm just falling!

Kathleen Luksza Morrissey

Happy Birthday JP!

Kissing Frogs

I told you once that I would try to do it your way...
for as long as it lasted!
And I really did try!
You did too, for awhile, I think!
You were so wonderful to be with...
when we were really together,
there was nothing better!
We just do not have the same wants or needs...
I am driving you crazy....you are driving me crazy!!!
It isn't a healthy relationship for either of us ...
It is so much more than you want...
And it is less than I need!
It is less than you want...
And more than I can do!
And this is as long as it's lasted!
If you have to "kiss a lot of frogs...
before you find your Prince" ...
Turns out maybe you are a frog...!

Kathleen Luksza Morrissey

Last Wish

We all have a last wish before we pass away
To behold that eternal peace on our last day,
As we were taught our first prayer
" Now I lay me down to sleep..."
We take comfort knowing the Lord will protect our soul to keep...
My wish before I die is simple, and it's this,
Please God grant me my final wish!
Please have my love to be near...
To give thanks for being my dear..
My last touch will be holding her hand,
Expressing how each feeling was grand!
My last sight will be of her beauty;
how she made me proud!
Never lost sight of her during our darkest times, or in a crowd...
My last words spoken will be from my heart,
Speaking in a whisper "loved you" from the start...
Yes, this is my wish before I die...
Hope God will grant my last goodbye..

James F. Plummer

Love Letter

If you only knew how wonderful you are!!!
You have the most off beat quirky, funny sense of humor!
You make me smile, you make me laugh, you make me feel,
... well you know how you make me feel!
You are staunch about what you believe is right or wrong...
How a baseball uniform should be worn!
Boycotting BP, ...and Catholic Popes...don't even get you started!
You are sweet and considerate, gentle and kind, sensitive, intelligent, honest...
You are a very good man...self taught...and I admire you immensely!
You are rough and demanding and drive me out of my mind!
You make me want you...in my body, in my life, in my world!
And so late in life...you finally developed this...
amazing taste in women!
Or did you?
When you go away, you make me feel so helpless...
I want to be able to give you what you need...
I want To fix it for you, when you are depressed and down,
I want my love for you to be enough to bring you around...
If I had a magic wand to wave...I'd make you always... content!
There would be an armor to protect you
from all the things that hurt, and worry you!
I love it when you talk, and it is a good thing...because you DO talk!
When you stop talking I get afraid... of what you might not be saying...
Sometimes I take it personally... and then I get a little crazy!
...As you've no doubt observed!
I am getting used to it though,
you go someplace dark and brooding for awhile...
It is so hard for me to accept that I can't fix it,
can't make the demons go away!
Space is what you say you need,
and I find it hard to give, hard to understand...
The romantic in me always thinks that love will find a way!
I am trying though! You are my love,
I miss you...And I just want to see you smile!

Kathy Morrissey

Memories

In my book of memories,
its pages now yellow and torn
Are all the golden memories
of past loves I have borne.
And with each memory I smile
until I come to you...
For that was the love that didn't stop
When you found someone new.
And though we've gone our separate ways
And we've drifted far apart,
There will always be a place for you,
In the corner of my heart.

Kathy Luksza Morrissey
STA 73

Monster

There is a monster at the gate,
Please don't let him in!
There is a monster
And he's waiting to consume me...
He'll eat my heart...
Get drunk on my tears!
His name is Grief...
And when he is through
My greatest fear
Is there will be nothing left...
Nothing left but mourning!
There is a monster at the gate!
His name is Grief, and
He's waiting to consume me...

Kathleen Luksza Morrissey

Normal

Getting back to normal,
to who I used to be...
Is that a place where I can go
when the pain has set me free?
Do I even remember how to be...normal?
Remember how to be that person?
When I only want to flee!
Normal was sanity, optimism, and hope!
Normal was happy, carefree, laughter!
Normal is now putting one foot before the other...
Normal is surviving one more day!
Will it ever be normal to live my life
Without you?

Kathleen Luksza Morrissey

Overflow

The day you were born I felt things I'd never known before!
The love that swelled within me was overwhelming!
My heart swelled to overflow...
All that I lived for was to protect you, keep you safe,
Hold you...hold onto you...and I didn't want to let you go!

You were the joy of my existence!
Our life...our family...our world...
You, your brother, your Dad, and me!
It was the best that life could ever be!
And I didn't want to let it go!

When you left the nest...when you flew away
All I could do was pray...and pray...and pray
that God would do
What I couldn't do for you anymore!
Protect you...keep you safe...

The day that you died I felt things I'd never known before!
The pain that swelled within me was overwhelming!
My heart swelled to overflow...
All I lived for was to protect you, keep you safe,
Hold you...hold onto you...and I didn't want to let you go!

Kathleen Luksza Morrissey
For my son, Terry Morrissey

Reflections

I gazed in the mirror and was amazed to see
the reflections of my life…looking back at me…

She was the little girl who I used to be!
Shy to a fault, lost in her books, in her dreams…
Always feeling a little off center,
Not quite comfortable being the child she should be!

She was the teenager, finally emerging from her shell…
Starting to feel comfortable in her own skin,
Dreaming of love…and happily ever after…
Anxious to be the woman she wanted to be!

She was the wife and the mother…
She'd finally found her place in life,
The dream had come true, it was her reality…
She was who she was supposed to be!

She was the widow, who couldn't believe
That happily ever after… was over!
The dream was a nightmare, and
She didn't know… if she wasn't a wife…who to be!

She was me…living my life, feeling a little off center…
Starting to feel comfortable… and know who I am
Learning to have hope…to dream again…
She was me starting over …learning to be…me!

And then the mirror shattered!

Kathleen Luksza Morrissey

Sisters of the Heart

I don't know what I would do without my sisters,
Each and every one!
The most special of course are my sibling sisters,
We share a lifetime of memories...
We share laughter and love, and secrets, and fun!
And we share our broken hearts!
And then of course there are my family sisters,
My in-laws and my nieces,
We share so many memories...
We share laughter and love, and secrets, and fun!
And we share our broken hearts!
And then there are my special sisters,
sisters of the heart...
My soul sisters, if you will...
We share so many memories...
We share laughter and love, and secrets, and fun!
And we share our broken hearts!
My broken heart could not survive,
I'll be the first to admit it...
If it weren't for my sisters...
And sharing, and caring!
We share laughter and love, and secrets!, and fun
And they mend my broken heart!

Kathleen Luksza Morrissey

Somebody Came

I never knew your name,
Your face, your cry,
I never felt a bullet
And I never had to die.
I'll never know if I'm to blame
Cause they gave a war
And somebody came!

Kathy Luksza Morrissey
STA, Class of 73

Sometimes

Sometimes in the night, when I'm drifting in that almost place,
I can almost feel you touch me, almost feel you...

Sometimes in the night, when I'm floating just beyond sleep,
I can almost hear your whisper, almost hear you...

Sometimes in the night, you wash your warmth over me,
you soak up my sadness with your smile...
I can almost feel happy, almost feel...

Sometimes I can feel you with me when I awaken,
And I can make it through a day without you...

For Jack – K. Morrissey

Steve

Right from the start
did you have a chance?
Life seemed to break your heart,
It was a tragic romance!

But you didn't seem to care,
And we didn't know you cried,
So it really seems unfair
That you gave up and died!

Death comes, and life goes on,
But for a moment we stop to cry
For a friend, now gone,
And forever we'll wonder why?

Kathy Luksza Morrissey
STA   73
Dedicated to my friend Steve Traw

The Antique Shop

We walked through the Antique Shop together, viewing someone else's past...
And I was amazed to see so many 'treasures' that reminded me of my own!
A trip down memory lane...inspired by a cookie cutter!
Easter and Christmas...Family gatherings!
The smell of turkey in the oven, children and magic...laughter and love!
Santa and the Bunny...trees hung with homemade ornaments, baskets filled with
Chocolate and jelly beans...and homemade sugar cookies, decorated with care...
Delicacies! Works of art!...
Consumed without the proper appreciation!
A past that was suddenly so alive I could smell it! Taste it!
And see the people who were there...hear their voices...
in that "Norman Rockwell" portrait type memory!
Days of old, loved ones, some gone, some grown!
And I can finally appreciate...
The master piece that was a cookie!

Kathleen Luksza Morrissey, 2010

For My Mother, Mary C. Milner Luksza
For my Mother In Law, Marie Geiger Morrissey

The Collectors Shop

I entered a collectors shop one Saturday afternoon just to browse around,
The shelves were full of items from the top of the wall going down to the
ground.

The shop was stocked with memorabilia from days that had long since passed
Toys, and books that were made for kids to enjoy back then, and were made
to last!

The collector had items all placed in alphabetical order from Airplanes that
once flew,
to numerous stuffed animals that we imagined in our adventurous minds
escaped from the Zoo

Oh, the shop held a magical presence as I further walked inside, looked, and
even touched..
For I knew all the toys wanted to come alive, be active once again ever so
much!

All of a sudden the store became dark, the doors locked, and shades on the
windows came down,
My ears heard strange sounds of toys winding, and my eyes saw the
movements of clowns..

Heard sound of trains chugging down the tracks, belching smoke from their
stacks into the air..
Even glanced over in the corner, and saw Raggedy Ann rocking on her
oversized chair!

All the music boxes were playing their tunes as the ballerinas danced in a
circle with elegance, and grace..
And yes, even the Prince was holding the Princess close to chest moving so
gracefully in a confined space!

Books all opened their covers, and began to speak the story which they were
written to tell..
Some told stories that made you smile, while others told stories which caused
your eyes to swell..

The dolls got together, dressed in clothes that ones mother made to place on
their back..
Even viewed Barbie dolls dressed with fancy tops, and wearing the latest
designer slacks..

Lunch boxes opened, and was curious to know what others had packed for
lunch..

They contained basically the same ,nothing fancy, drink, sandwich, and chips
to munch..

Saw puppets jumping into the air with delight for they were way too idle not
full of life..
Full of joy, and amusement for it was their purpose to bring needed smiles,
never strife..

Cap pistols fired blank shots into the air,
While bows shot plastic tip arrows across the sky..
Toy soldiers that were playing war did not know if they would return from
battle , or to die..

The board games were laying on tables along with cards, and dice..
Even noticed stuffed cats chasing the rubber mice..

Life filled the air it was every where you looked around..
The toys made it all beautiful with their lights and sounds..

Without warning a knock bellowed on the wood door of the collectors store..
The toys all became silent again, but in a brief moment had played once
more..

We all once have been children, and had toys that brought us joy, and
pleasure..
So when life gets you down take a trip the collectors store, and once again
view God's treasure..

James F. Plummer

The Memory Still Lingers

There were red roses
And I was so young!
We kissed each other slowly
And loves words were sung.

It ended sometime later,
With war you were gone...
I thought I'd die without you;
But life kept going on...

Now, so many years later
I know it might be wrong,
But the memory still lingers...
Of a kiss and an old, old song.

Kathy Luksza Morrissey

STA 73

The Mirror

I entered a local bar, and sat on a stool that was unoccupied,
No one sitting to the left, nor anyone sitting on the right side.

In front of me was located a mirror placed in front of the bar,
Could view many people in the place whether they were near or far..

Bartender approached asked "what would be your drink of choice" ?
"Oh, just a beer for now", but deep inside I needed a voice..

I peered into that mirror that was in front of me..
And soon an old man sat down, and placed his hand on my knee..

I stayed focused, peering into the mirror, and never turned my head..
My ears just listened to the words the old man had said..

How did he know what my thoughts were, and how I lived my life?
Hell, he knew about my childhood, and the number of ex-wives..

Money can be spent on material belongings, and tomorrow will be
thrown away..
But the love you spend with that special one now will be there day
after day..

Always stand tall like an oak that's blowing into the wind..
Never let a storm break your branches, allowing only to bend..

Live the day you awoke to as though it will be the last..
Look forward to the next hour, and not the hours that had past..

Never become lost in the dark... for the moons glow will shine you a
direction
And as the sunrises, it will guide you, and will make the necessary
corrections..

I turned my head to view the old man face to face..
No one was sitting there, just an empty stool in its place..

Bartender asked "You okay, for it seems as though you got lost in your
drink"
I'm okay, just heard what my heart has felt forever so long, and had
time to think..

Today we are young, and we really can't see ourselves in our mirrors..
But tomorrow will soon come, and the lives we've lived will become
ever clearer..

James F. Plummer

The Only Couple

You didn't know when we met
that I was suffering a broken heart!
How could you?
I laughed, and teased and flirted...
And then we danced!
The only couple on the floor!
I didn't know when we met
that you were a lonely man!
How could I?
You laughed and teased and flirted...
And then we danced!
The only couple on the floor!
We danced and we laughed...
and we danced some more!
My heart was mending...
you weren't as lonely as before!
And from now on...
As long as the music doesn't stop...
We will dance, and we will laugh,
and we will dance some more...
And we will always be
The only couple on the floor!

Kathy Morrissey

For Art

The Rescue

She was a princess, trapped in a tower of loneliness
Waiting for a prince to save her from despair,
To yield his glowing sword and slay the enemy!
To be strong and worthy...To be a knight to save her life!
To quench her thirst, And satisfy her hunger...
She prayed for rescue and searched for solace...
Please dear Lord, don't let me be trapped forever!

He was a prince, lost in the forest,
Searching, wondering if he'd ever find his way...
Was there a way out of this place he'd wandered into,
Could he prove that he was strong still, and worthy?
Was there someone who could quench his thirst and satisfy his hunger...
He prayed for rescue and searched for solace...
Please dear Lord, don't let me be lost forever!

He saw the tower in the distance, and galloped, anxiously...
Hoping someone there might help him find his way!

She sensed his coming! Could it be!
Might there be someone who can rescue me!
She prayed he'd see her, and know what he must do...

He scaled the tower and held out his hand,
He thrust his sword to slay the enemy...and he WAS strong and worthy!
He fed her hunger, he quenched her thirst, he touched her heart!

She mounted his steed, and together a new journey began...
Will she lead him from the forest, and help him find his way?
She prayed he'd see her and she'd know what she must do...

To satisfy his hunger, to quench his thirst...and touch his heart
To have the might to save his life!
And be strong and worthy, too...

They prayed for rescue and searched for solace...and Please dear Lord...

Kathy Morrissey
Happy Valentines Day, JP

Therapy

They think I need grief counseling, therapy...
Do they think that it can fix me?
Is it supposed to make the pain go away,
make me forget how much I loved you?
I don't want to forget...
I can stand the pain!
You were worth it!
All the joy you gave me for all of your life
Sustains me now,
The memories of laughter,
of the uniqueness of you...
Of us...our family!
It was so special, a treasure...
To keep in my heart, hold onto forever!
It is the therapy of my soul to remember!

For my husband, Jack Morrissey
For my son, Terry Morrissey

Kathleen Luksza Morrissey

Trivia

Singing in bed, flowers in an ice storm,
anything wrapped in bacon!
The trivia of our story!
Blueberry Hill...Chuck Berry's Thrill,
and ours...for your birthday!
The trivia of our story!
Memphis in May, Jerry Lee...Great Balls of Fire!
Running from storms! And Graceland!
The trivia of our story!
Bar b q, and baseball games,
Super Bowl and wing dip!
Multi-tasking!
The trivia of our story!
Sitcoms and old movies that we never quite saw...
The trivia of our story!
Passion and touching, needing, desire...
feeling so young again!
The trivia of our story!
Talking about everything! And talking some more!
teasing and laughing and...senior moments...
The trivia of our story!
Lost memories, lost words, lost hope...
lost innocence, lost love...goodbyes...
You were the King of Trivia...
In our story!

Kathleen Luksza Morrissey

Victim of Conviction

Never taught you the right way...
We all got to make our own mistakes!
Don't know if all can be forgiven...
Given a choice I'll make the wrong decision!
Burn bridges before ever crossing!
I know we'll never be more than friends...
At times even less,
You don't feel like talking!
You know when I party, I party serious!
Desperate times don't seem so desperate
Desperate times don't seem so desperate
Desperate times don't seem so desperate!!!!

Lyrics by Shaun Morrissey
For The Humanoids

When We First Meet

When we first met, you profiled me and
I e-mailed you...
When we first met, I told you my problems
And you shared yours...
When we first met you sent a poem you'd written,
I promised to do the same...
But I don't know what makes you laugh,
and you don't know how I look...
I don't know where you grew up, or about your family,
and you don't know my favorite book...
But I do know you have a cute little convertible
And I do know that you like baseball,
And I do know that you are a passionate romantic
And I do know that you fall in love easily...
and maybe out of love too!
When we first meet, what then?

Kathy Morrissey

When We First Met

When we first met, I didn't know that I would even kiss you,
And I didn't know that I would like ...you ... so much! so fast!
Too fast!
But I do know that I like being with you,
and that when I'm not...I miss you!
And I do know that you can cook!!!
And that you're a good son,
And I do know that I like your smile, your laughter, your looks
(and did I mention that you can uh... cook!)
But did you know that I too am a romantic who might fall too easily,
And it scares me ...
Because my Jimmy, my lover, my man...
You have the power to thrill me, to hurt me, to please me, to...
When we next meet, what then?

Kathy Morrissey

When We Last Met

When we first met
I thought you fell in love easily,
and maybe out of love too...
I didn't know though...
that I would fall so in love with you!
I told you from the start that you had the power to...
And you did thrill me,
you did please me...
and you did hurt me...
Maybe I'd seen it coming from the start!
When we last met, you took my pride...
And Jimmy, my love, you broke my heart!
I wonder...will we ever meet again?

Kathleen Morrissey

Meeting

We just keep meeting...
We can never say goodbye!
You say you don't want to be together,
You say I'd be better off with another...
I am not who you need,
I can't satisfy your desire!
I try to let you go...
Try to love another...
And you say you want to meet me!
No matter how hard we try
We are drawn to each other!
Am I not who you need
To satisfy your desire?
Just one more time...
Before we say goodbye...forever!
Will we ever stop meeting?
And when we do, what then?

Kathleen Morrissey

The Yardstick

My Dad was my first hero,
and he will always be
the yardstick with which I measure...
if you are good enough for me!
He was strong and smart and clever!
He was funny as could be!
And he could tell a story...make me laugh
Better than anyone...
Till Jack!
He loved baseball and football...
democracy and integrity,
music and trivia!
And he could explain it all to me...
Better than anyone...
Till Jimmy!
He loved to dance, and was romantic
and sweet
And could make me feel pretty
and graceful and smart
Better than anyone...
Till Art!
He loved people and beer, and food, laughter and fun...
And he loved his family!
And if I've ever loved you a little, or a lot...
It's because there is something in you
that reminds me of My Dad...
He was my first hero,
and he will always be
the yardstick with which I measure...
if you are good enough for me!

For my Dad, Louis Luksza
Kathleen Luksza Morrissey

You Deny

I am everything you ever needed...
your hearts desire...
And yet you say that we can never be!
You deny your heart...I don't know why
You deny your love...
I am everything you ever wanted,
your body is on fire!
And yet you say that we can never be!
You say I'm not enough...
You need variety!
You can't deny the way you feel...
when you are touching me,
and yet you deny that we are meant to be!
You deny the total compatibility!
You say it is physical, only physical...
And your heart doesn't feel it!
I am everything you ever needed,
and yet you deny...even the possibility !

Kathy Morrissey

You Taught Me

You taught me to laugh and
Laughter filled the corners of our world

You taught me to love and
Love filled the places in our hearts

You taught me to live and
Living with you made life worth living

Because you taught me, I can laugh, I can love,
I can almost live...without you!

Kathy Morrissey
For Jack

You Tell Me

You tell me that you love me,
you have almost from the start...
I think you are smitten,
and don't know your heart!
I tell you that I like you...a lot!
And it is too soon
To know if I will love you...
but I like you, you goon!
I don't want you to love,
not now, not yet!!!
There are so many things
I am still trying to get!
My emotions are churning
My feelings are mixed...
I like being with you,
But I'm not ready to commit!

Kathy Morrissey